Barry the Butter Blob

discovers

The Meaning of Life

by Ann Louise Stubbs

Crombie Jardine
PUBLISHING LIMITED

13 Nonsuch Walk, Cheam, Surrey, SM2 7LG
www.crombiejardine.com

First published by
Crombie Jardine Publishing Limited in 2006

ISBN 1-905102-55-0

Written & illustrated by Ann Louise Stubbs

Designed by www.glensaville.com
Printed & bound in Belgium by Proost

for Rick

Barry the Butter Blob
was generally a
happy kinda guy...

But today he was not
feeling his usual chirpy
self...

He asked himself,
"What is the Meaning of Life?"

...but he could not
find the answer...

He also felt really <u>afraid</u>,
because he knew that
breakfast time would
come sooner or later...

...and <u>that</u> was a really
frightening thought for a
butter blob...

...and because he was
feeling down in the dumps
he just wasn't getting a
<u>kick</u> out of his friends
anymore...

There was Burt the Broccoli,
who had always been a good
buddy, but was really <u>bossy</u>
and always pushing
Barry around...

now, when we are on
the plate make sure
<u>you</u> stay on the side!

Then, there was Alfred, the annoyingly optimistic aubergine, who, <u>no</u> <u>matter</u> <u>what</u> <u>had</u> <u>happened</u>, always managed to see the positive side of <u>everything</u>...

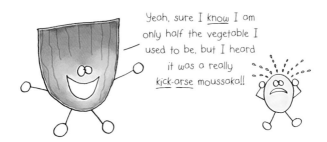

Yeah, sure I <u>know</u> I am only half the vegetable I used to be, but I heard it was a really <u>kick-arse</u> moussaka!!

...and of course Elaine the Egg, who really did have a heart of gold, but could be <u>hyper-sensitive</u> and could read something into nothing...

You know Barry the other day, when you asked me how I was? What <u>exactly</u> did you mean by that?

sheeeesh!

...and finally, Clarence the Cucumber who could be really interesting to talk to, that is, when he wasn't harping on about his Ph.d. in Romantic Poetry...

Barry was <u>fed</u> <u>up</u> with all
of them!
So he decided to hang out
by himself for a little while...

The <u>first</u> thing he did was get himself some new gimmicks to cheer himself up...

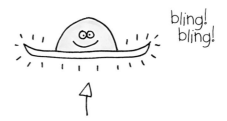

bling!
bling!

like a brand-new
state-of-the-art
butter tray!

...but this only made him
happy for a while...

...then

he

was

bored...

So <u>then</u> he tried to live life
dangerously
to get some more <u>excitement!</u>

→ like standing too close
to the hot kettle...

...but this only gave him a cheap <u>thrill</u> and he always felt awful afterwards...

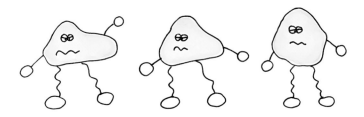

...or sometimes (just for a laugh)
he would balance on the
edge of a hot saucepan...

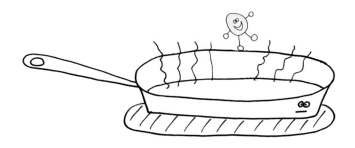

...but after a couple of
close calls with a fish slice
and a pancake he decided
not to do that anymore...

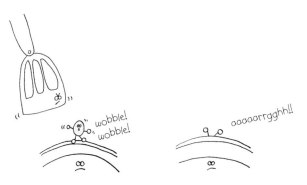

...or occasionally, if he was feeling particularly <u>reckless</u> he would go and make faces at Terence the Toast ('cos he was <u>such</u> a square)...

...but when Terence
brought along the other
slices it didn't seem like
such a good idea after all...

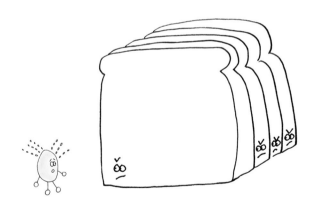

As time went by
he got tired of fooling
around

?

...but he couldn't
decide what to do next!

...so he went back
to his butter tray
to <u>chill</u> <u>out</u>...

...and after a little while
of sitting there alone...

...he began to meditate to
look for the _real_ blob within...

...and he meditated for
quite a long time
(for a butter blob)...

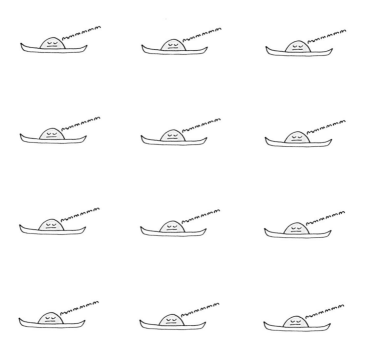

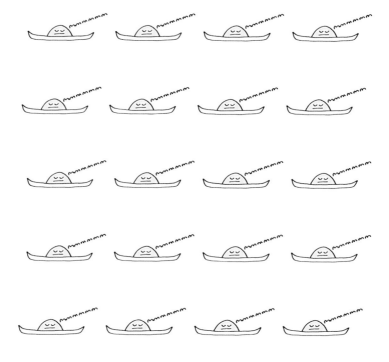

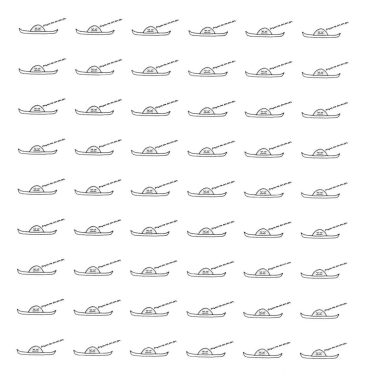

...then something wonderful happened...

He realised that
everything was already
perfect exactly as
it was!!!

...and that included <u>himself</u>, and everyone else in the fridge...

...and then he started to
remember all the <u>good</u> times
he had shared <u>with his</u>
friends...

...like the time Burt had stood up for him when all the Brussel sprouts had ganged up on him...

...and how Alfred could make
him laugh so hard he thought
he would <u>melt</u> with all his
crazy jokes about kitchen
utensils...

...Cosy evenings with Clarence
in the vegetable compartment
debating the merits of organic
versus genetically modified vegetable
production in the post-modernist
movement of vegetable ethics...

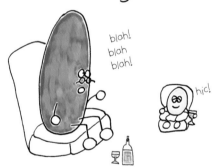

...and romantic moments watching the fridge light turn off with Elaine...

...and suddenly he was
filled with
<u>B</u>ig <u>W</u>arm <u>W</u>onderful
feelings of <u>Love</u>!!!

...and there was <u>so</u> <u>much</u> love that warm golden buttery love flowed out from the fridge to fill up the <u>whole</u> <u>kitchen</u>...

...and all the appliances rejoiced!!

To celebrate, he decided to throw
a <u>fantastic party</u>, with lots of
loud music, ice sculptures and
cocktails and he invited all
his friends!!

He danced all night with Elaine
to his favourite Dusty Springfield
tracks and everyone had
a fantastic time...

...and when breakfast time
finally came, Barry felt so
.peaceful and happy.
that he was completely
one with the toast...

...and very
gradually
he began
to melt
from the
warmth
of the
toast...

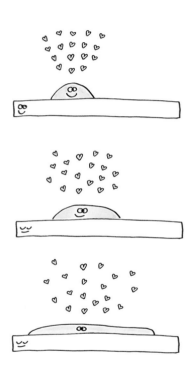

...until he completely...

♡

disappeared !!

Terence the Toilet

Travels The World

by Ann Louise Stubbs

Also available by Ann Louise Stubbs

1-905102-53-4 · £4.99

www.crombiejardine.com

www.annlouisestubbs.co.uk